FOREVER HAUNTED

D.E. Gould

authorHOUSE®

AuthorHouse™
1663 Liberty Drive
Bloomington, IN 47403
www.authorhouse.com
Phone: 1-800-839-8640

First published by AuthorHouse 9/23/2009

ISBN: 978-1-4490-2973-9 (sc)

Printed in the United States of America
Bloomington, Indiana

This book is printed on acid-free paper.

CONTENTS

PROLOGUE

There it stood. Like it had stood so many years ago. The long wooded porch, that we used to roller skate on. The boards warped with age. The faded gray paint, that had cracked and withered. From all the long and cold winter nights, that it had went through. But yet it still stood, the old house. It was almost like a beacon through time. Drawing me back as if it held some type of power over me. Inside the house was the same. Some how time had almost stood still for me. There was the front room, the two bedrooms. Off to one side, the bathroom straight ahead of the kitchen at the other end.

There in the small room, where once three girls slept. The room that held me so scared. So many years ago. What was so terrifying about it? The old closet wasgone. Was it the closet? Was it the way the clothes hung in it? The boxes stacked on top. The way the light hit it making the shadows fade in and out? Causing it to look like someone was hiding in it. And there it was again, a single sob. A child's sob. A child who never felt their parent's arm around them. Who had never been comforted. Then the anger that had ate at the house, bit by bit, until the whole house was digested. By the anger.

The awful memories, which came flooding back to my mind. As if a dam broke, and suddenly released its contents. The harsh words, wildly spoken to us. The threats of having us taken to a state home. The wild look in his eyes, as he would dish out his punishments.

Foronly things he swore we had done. The screams still echoing through the small house. The sounds of his hand hitting our small bodies. Could it be I still could hear it over the muffled cries, of smaller children. The constant abuse, the hate, the sobs. This happened in my family. But what if it happened before, and before, and before? After all the house was over a hundred years old.

THE MORGAN HOUSE

The first time that I experienced a ghost was when I was only five years old. It was during the time my grandma Callahan was alive. About 1957, we were living up in Morgan, Utah. The community of Enterprise. There were about six families at the time. Grandma came up from Salt Lake City, to see us. She always slept with me.

The old gray home was almost a hundred years old, at the time. My family was the one of the first dysfunctional families. I had just gotten to sleep, when grandma whispered in my ear.

"Darlene," then she shook me just to make sure. "Darlene, can you hear those people in the front room?" I remember being so tired that I could hardly even talk. "Yes, grandma." We laid and listened to the men talk about insurance, and other subjects. And there were woman also talking. At some point during the night, I had fallen asleep. In the warm bed, that the heat from the two bodies had created. And then it was gone, asif someone had come along and stolen the warmth from the bed. And left me with the cold instead.

A few moments later I could hear my dad yelling at someone, and then as if the whole world had stopped. And the world as I once knew it, came to a sudden end. My dad yelled my name. "Darlene!" "Darlene, get in here now!" I slowly touched the icy floors with my bare feet. And tried to make them take steps across the cold floor. I knew for some reason, I was in really big trouble. And chances where I was about to get my butt kicked, for something I had no idea of what I had done.

There in the kitchen was grandma, mom, and dad. Grandma was yelling how we had heard the party going on last night. And how she wasn't good enough to even be invited to the party.

Then it was my moms turn in trying to tell grandma that there was no party, going on and that she must have been asleep and dreamed it all. Then grandma turned to me and said:" tell them about all of the talking going on last night, we heard in the front room?" I looked up at grandma, andthen over to my dad. I knew I had to tell the truth.

"We did hear voices last night, and we listened for a long time." That was all it took. My father raised his hand and slapped me for lying. Grandma never came to our house again. The voices were only just beginning. A couple of years later my cousin, Gary from California had come to live with us. His parents couldn't handle him, and so they thought my dad could. The time that Gary spent at our home, I can only remember only once that the house had come to life. And for a kid from California once was enough.

It all started the night that my parents decided to go out, and be alone without he kids tagging along. What I remember, that we were all in the front room, and the lights were out in the front room. And only the kitchen light was on. We were watching Wagon Train.

It was a popular TV series. In the late 50's early 60's. And we were all enthralled with what was happening on the TV. So no one noticed the house starting to come to life. No one noticed the little girls giggling in the kitchen. When that didn't get our attention, the plates started to softly rattle. And asno one paid attention to that. The noise started to get louder and louder, until it sounded as if the stack of plates were about to fall off the shelf that they were stacked on.

With that, the noise awakened Gary. To what was going on in the kitchen. It was as if he thought that his pants were on fire. Because he leaped out of the chair, that he was so comfortable in. And leaped at least two feet in the air, screaming. "What the hell was that?" There before my eyes, my tough cousin transformed from this tough smart mouthed kid, into my knight in shinning armor. All the while the dishes, along with the pots and pans, banging so loud I thought the neighbors would hear it. Gary gathered us all up and pulled us into the kitchen, and told us to get under the kitchen table. He then ran over to the knife drawer, and took out the butcher knives, and put them inside of his belt. Getting himself ready for the fight of his life.

2

What he was going to fight, I don't know. But he turned to face us. And yelled in the air:" come and get me!" At that point, I don't know who was laughing the hardest, us under the table or the sound of the little ghost girl. But there he stood ready to defent us, from what ever unseen forces. As it had started it stopped. Gary went back to California. Grandma died a couple of years later, and the day we moved from the house. The baby cried, the little girl laughed. And oh, yes the insurance men and their woman started to talk once again.

We had onl heard the cry of the baby a few times, and it wasn't as if we could do anything to comfort it. I never saw Gary again. I always wondered what he thought about that night. I have often thought about the sounds of the old Morgan house. After all it was one hundered years old in the fifties. A lot of people lived and died in that house. A couple of years ago, I went to see the old place. Its still standing, and I even went up and knocked on the door. An elderly woman answered the door, it wasn't the same. I couldn't hear the baby's cry, or the little girl laughing.It was like the ghosts had finally moved on.

THE VOICE

Trudy would never see the age of five. Karen would die in her fortines, this chapter is for them. During the early sixties, there was no 911. Things that went on in the home, stayed in our home.

No one was to tell secrets, always secrets. No one tells. It was a cold April moring, and the rain clouds hung low over the mountains, and on the foot hills. Mom said, if she felt better by lunch we could go to the bank. And open me up a savings account, to help save my babysitting money. I was to call her at lunch. School went fast, but when your in junior high, that's an experience in its self.

Luch came by, and I called home. And no one anwered. As I heard the last bell of the day, I knew something was wrong. I went to my locker and shoved my books into it. I ran half a mile home, over the foot hills down to my home. I remember touching the door knob, until I finally reached out and grabbing it firmly. Opening up the door, there inside of the house we had just moved into from Morgan. I saw Danny on the hide a bed in the front room. I tried to wake him up, and is all he would do is open his eyes. Looking around as if he was searching for the far away voice. Then he closed them. I got some paper towels, and wiped the foam that was bubbling out from his mouth. I went into our bedroom, and there laid Karen and mom. They were in the same condition as Danny. I went into the kitchen, and started to look through mom's telephone book. There was a list of doctors. Doctors that we couldn't pay the bills, to which one mom was seeing. Which one did she not see, due to non payment. There was Connie's name, I tried calling her. She was the oldest, but living in Texas. But she was still at work. I even tried to call Max at school.

But the person who answered the phone, said the pa system would not be heard over the game. My dad, he was always up at the cabin.

It had no services. I was starting to panic, as to what to do. But a very calm feeling came over me. And I knelt down and prayed. I asked what to do? In to time I had gotten the voice. The voice told me to open all the doors and windows in the house. As fast as I could, I did just that. A half an hour later I shut the house up, and I went babysittitng. Remember what goes on in the family, stays in the family.

Max my oldest brother, finally came home. He called me and asked what to do? Only one hour before, I didn't know what or who to call? I told him you've got to call doctor Rogers. Max did that. And when the doctor said, call me back in a hour. Max said the most important thing, he would ever say. "What about the foam coming out of their mouths?" The doctor got a hold of the ambulance, and the fire engines, that carried the oxygen. They rushed them off to the hospital. The doctor was getting the paper work in order to transfer Trudy and Danny to the children's ward. When a nurse came up and told doctor Rogers, that Trudy had died. From that point, the doctor gave the family no hope for the rest of the to recover.

Connie went and made arrangements for four coffins, to be bought. Karen laid in a coma, for almost three months. When she came out of the coma, she had to learn how to walk again. One night while we were laying in bed. She told me of a dream she had. And it was in that dream, she knew Trudy had died. She says she was on the steps of a stair case, with a light. Trudy and her. Along with a man dressed in white. He was walking with them up the stairs. When he turned to her, and told her to go back down the stairs. It wasn't her time.

There was about 1 ½ minutes she had no pulse. My family had Carbon Monoxide poisoning. The furnace backed up, and the gas had gone up to the ceiling. And was coming back down, and when it hit the floor the house would explode. It would of killed all of them. And not just Trudy. The fire chief asked my dad, a couple of weeks after what happened. "Who opened up the house, and aired it out?"

"That would have been Darlene, that dumb kid, instead of calling for help. She does that sir." The fire chief said:" I wouldn't call her dumb. No one can tell what Carbon Monoxide gas smells like."

"Because its ordor less. Not even I would of known that's what was wrong by just walking into a house. She gave us time to get here." I told people of why I opened the house. The worst judge of me was my parents, and my aunt Thisby. Aunt Thisby told me I received the wrong message. After that I stopped telling people for over forty years, until now. I was a young girl, who knelt down and asked God, what to do? And the voice told me what to do. I didn't question the voice? I did what it said. I still hear that voice, now and again. Karen, died four years ago. She now haunts my home. She peeks around the corner of things for only a second.

My New Life

When I was twenty one years old, I met a young man named Raymond Robert Gould. We were married the same month I turned 22. Ray didn't belive in ghosts, until he met me. He moved into a small one bedroom apartment. He spent a total of one night, before leaving. On his first night in the apartment he awoke with someone stroking his arm. He found another apartment to move into.

A few years later Elizabeth was born. And another gifted child entered the world. We didn't experience much until Elizabeth was six years old. We had just moved back from Coopville, Washington.

Both me and Ray was working for a cleaning services. We had four hours to clean the City and County Building. I was in the City and County Building where the ghosts started to come alive, once again. We had an office that had to be done first, due to the fact there was no lights. The building was built in 1800's, so the ceiling was our light. It had a big bay windows. It was a drafting room, and is all we had do was empty the garbage cans. And vacuum the floor in twenty minutes. While I would empty the garbage, Ray would vacuum. So I went through and emptied all of the cans. And when Ray came through with the vacuum, at the end of the drafting tables. There was the garbage thrown all over the floor.

"Ray asked me if I had forgotten the garbage over here?" "I told him, no." But the garbage was all over here. " Does it have chicken bones in it? Because the garbage I picked up had chicken bones." Ray couldn't even talk. But there were the chicken bones in over here in the garbage. We cleaned up the mess, and went down to the elevator. To take it down to the first floor, where the emptied the trash bags.

While we were in the elevator waiting for the first floor, we started to hear voices. As if a group of office people were waiting for the slow elevator, to reach their floor. Me and Ray looked at each other, and we both spoke togther. "What the hell!" The elevator doors slowly opened to an empty hall. No one ins sight. We stepped out from the elevator, and no one was either left or right.

We took our garbage out and dumped it. And then we found the security guard. We all sat down in the closest office, and we began to tell him. It all started with the garbage up on the third floor, reappearing as if we didn't gather it up. Then when we was coming down the elevator, we heard voices in the hall. But there was no one in there. The guard began to tell us. "Well you see, the room on the third floor belonged to one contractor. Who could draw with the best. He doesn't like new people in his room. So he throws garbage around the floor, and sometimes he will unroll the large scrolls and toss them. "Then what of the voices we heard, as we got off the elevator?" Ray asked. "Well!" "We all of the guards has discussed it, and when ever we have heard it. It sounded like a bunch of office workers talking, am I right?" We just looked at him and told, him yes. We found better jobs, ones that didn't involve ghosts. It had been three, Liz was nine years old and going to school. It was on one of those spring days, that the flowers were just starting to bloom. When it started all over again. We had a knock at our front door, and it was a plain clothes detective. That was standing there. He wanted to know about the woman who lived across the street from us. If we had seen her or anyone with her, during the weekend?

We didn't know her very well, cause of our work hours. It was then that Liz and her friends walked up, and asked what was going on? Up until then Liz showed no signs of having any talents, like I had. Except for the two words she first spoke och no. Not mamma or dadda, but och no. We found out is a Scottish term for oh, no. And the policeman turned to her, and in a wrong way of asking Liz, did you see that lady across the street honey? This weekend?

Liz looked across the street, and looked up at the policeman. Then looked across the street, then returned her gaze at him, and very calmly said yes. She is standing right there, can't you go and ask her yourself? And with that she turned, and walked into the house.

Without missing a beat. The cop slowly turned around as if to see her, standing there. When of course there was no one there. The woman still laid in her basement, on the floor with iron lying beside her. Where the man had dropped it, when he had finished stabbing her to death with it. The cop left without saying a word. I asked Liz later, how come she could see the lady? And the cop couldn't? She said, because mommy we are alike.

THE DREAMS BEGIN

We moved to Magna, Utah. Shortly after the death of the lady. But who could blame us, most of the neighbors were leaving after that. After moving into the Magna house. I knew we had something in the basement. Whether or not if Liz noticed, she had not told me yet. On October 28th, Liz called one of her friends in West Jordan. And she got the worst call of her life. Her friend told her that her brother was killed in an accident. It crushed Liz, not only that he died, he died on her birthday. Which was a few days before.

She came to me the next day and said, John was in her room and just stared at her and then he left. I guess he was there to tell her good-bye. I felt for Liz, because this was her second ghost sighting, and it would not be her last. At least it was a good friend. It was a few years later, and a week before Christmas. Liz came to me and said, she had a terrible dream. She said that she was looking at a list of names on a clipboard. And she found her grandma's name (Ray's mom) on the list. And scanned over to the right of her name and it said: Henrietta Gould died of heart failure.

I told her it was just a dream, and forget about it. I wished I listened to her, if I did I might have been able to get Ray prepared of the death that would come in a week. The night of December 21th, Henrietta went into the hospital, with part of her intestines that had died. The next day they performed the operation. The doctor came out and told us, that they didn't think she would have much of a chance to live outside of a nursing home. I went back to the dream Liz had, and thought she said she would die of heart failure, and when will that be? I prayed ot God, it would be soon. Because I knew Henrietta, would never live inone of those homes. Me, Ray, and Liz decided to go home, and come back in the morning. It was about two o' clock in the morning, of December 23. All of the sudden I could smell coffee being heated up, and toast was burning in the toaster. Before I start this story, I should tell you nobody in my family drinks coffee, only Henrietta did. And about this time she would get up and have her morning coffee, and bang cards on the table. I rolled over and told Ray, to go tell his mother to stop playing the cards! Then all of the sudden I remembered Henrietta was in the hospital, and I knew she died. At that moment the phone rang, and it was Ray's sister to tell us that she had died. When we got to the hospital, Ray's sister had told us her heart had given out. I thanked God that he took her, but then that damn dream came creeping back to me. Liz's dream had come true. The death of Henrietta, just about killed Ray. Henrietta and him were very close, as was Liz. I know it killed her to know the dream had come true. To have a dream of a loved one die. I can't even believe how painful that was for Liz, to have it come true. Now she talks to Henrietta in her dreams, and I feel that its not the same to have it in the flesh and blood. But to be able to talk to her after death, it helps because she can talk to her and find out about the family. She has met her great grandma on Ray's side, but what did it for me is when she talked to Trudy. That made me so thankful that she has this gift.

THE HEADLESS GHOST

During the 1920's until the late 1940's, Salt Air was an amusement park. It was built on the shores of the Great Salt Lake, just outside of Salt Lake City, Utah. There was a large band stand that housed a large dance floor, to which many came to either listen or dance to the music. There were few rides, but mostly was the lake. The lake's salt content was more concentrated then the oceans. So you could float standing up. One night someone set fire to Salt Air. Many rumors at the time around as to who would do such a thing. Some of the people got caught in the blaze, no one never knew how many or who they were. But then years after Salt Air was no more, and the rumors had died. Another Salt Air was built, but as luck would have it, it never really got off the ground. The lake rose that year. The lake was always rising and falling. But this year it flooded every where, it went beyond its normal flood lines, it flooded Salt Air. The damge was great.

A few summers past and the lake receded back to its old levels to when the first Salt Air was built.

The summer was unusually hot. It was on one of these hot nights, that Liz and her best friend Cheri decided to go out to the lake and go play in the water. They started out in the after noon, wading up to their knees in the water. And as young girls will, talked about nothing until dark. Still walking in the cool of the lake.

It was just as the full moon had rose over the mountains, that they realized they could no longer see the truck in sight. So they each decided that one would go North and the other would go South. And when they saw the truck, they would turn on the lights and honk the horn. And the other one would turn around and come. Liz took to the South, while Cheri took to the North. Liz started to walk towards

Salt Air. There in front of her was an old abandoned car, that had rusted out over the years. And then came the cement building that once been the electric house, for Salt Air all those years ago. It had seen better days. The only light she had was the moon light, to light her way. Meanwhile Cheri was almost to her truck. She could see it in the moon's light, and she knew if she could get to her truck safely. She could get Liz, in just a few minutes. Then all of these thoughts of being raped, and killed on the beach would not stop going threw her head. Liz turned to see if she could see Cheri. But it was to dark. Liz slowly walked down the beach, Liz knew she was getting closer to the Salt Air. When in front of her down the road, appeared to be a person with its head bent forward trying to see where it was going. After a few minutes of walking, Liz could see that he was was wearing a one piece bathing suit. She thought that, that was strange. So she yelled out, " hello could you help me?" But there was no answer. But as it got a little bit closer, she could see the stripes of the bathing suit.

It was like the pictures in Salt Air, of the bathing suits, the men wore. So Liz called out again. "Sir, can you help me?" But as the man came closer to Liz, she froze in her tracks and watched as the man passed her by. She couldn't believe what she has just seen. So he turned around and watched the man in the 19020's bathing suit walked into the darkness. And faded out of sight. " The man had no head!" " The man had no head!!" Liz kept on saying it out loud as if to convince anyone or maybe even herself. That the man who had passed her didn't have a head. It was only minutes later that Cheri, drove up to Liz. Liz got into the truck, Liz asked Cheri if she had seen anyone? And Cheri, said:"no."

Liz and Cheri never went back to the Great Salt Lake again. But who could blame them. Does the headless man still walk the beach at night? When Liz came home that night, she was so white. I didn't know she had a sun burn. She told me of the story.

CONNIE'S HOUSE

It took longer for us to drive from the airport than it did to fly from Las vegas. It was 8:00 pm Texas time, before we arrived at Connie's house. She is my oldest sister, and Johnny's her husband. She has two girls, Rachel and Leilani. It was getting late and Johnny and Connie was used to getting up early, and so we stayed up. We sat in the window seat, looking down the long dark hallway. The girls were out in the hot tub, me and Liz, we were recalling the day. We noticed that there was a mist forming at the end of the hallway. All of the doors to the three bedrooms were closed. So not to let any light escape in the dark hallway. As we sat glued to our seats, in fear as we watched the mist slowly find its way up the back of the hallway, towards an oval mirror. At that point we both looked at each other, with a half whisper voice: I told her to get her camera. She replied:" they are both in the dinning room table." I thought, oh shit! We both rose at the same time, and started to walk towards the dinning room that led to the dark hallway. Where all the mist was slowly rising to the oval mirror. We grabbed the cameras, as we held onto each other scared out of our wits. We walked slowly down the hall, I felt like I was on one of those movies. Where the hall goes on forever and forever without an end. I fell back of Liz, and started to film with the camcorder. Over her shoulder and it left her with a clear to shoot the pictures as fast as her camera would shoot.

We had slowly passed the first bedroom door, and was only ten feet from the mist. When all of the sudden Johnny came out and in of a sort of yell:" WHAT THE HELL ARE THE TWO OF YOU DOING?"

Liz and me just about jumped ten feet in the air, and I think Liz's hair went gray at that moment. I know I got a few new grays. At that moment, when Johnny came out the mist was gone. Liz had started to explain to Johnny what was going on. Because at that time all I could get out was a new alien language. Johnny just turned around shaking his head at us, and left us in the hallway by ourselves.

I told Liz, perhaps it is time to go to bed. I slept in one of the bedrooms, and Liz got the couch in the living room. I thought on how in the world was I going to be able to go to sleep.

But poor Liz, by herself in the living room. Liz got the couch, as she tried to close her eyes, she could feel someone watching over her. So she just stayed awake the night. When the sun had started to come up, she felt safe to finally close her eyes. Just as she started to sleep, aunt Connie and uncle Johnny had got up and started to make breakfast at 6:00 am. So she got up, and had breakfast with them. With only maybe an hour of sleep. This happened every night that we were at the house, no sleep for poor Liz. The next day we went and got the film developed, and there in the mirror was a mist in the shape of a woman's head. That was the only beginning for us.

That night it got a lot worse. Me, Liz, Rachel, and Leilani sat around in the front room. A small breeze seem to gently blow through the room cooling off the room. Following that was a scent of rose perfume, the scent went from one person to the other. As if to greet us to the house. And then it was gone. We all smelt the perfume and the cool breeze. It was getting late, and me and Liz was tired. But was the night went on, and on for Liz. Liz came into the room and woke me up, and asked if she could sleep on the floor? Soshe made up a bed and I went back to sleep. But poor Liz would not get any sleep tonight.

Liz just started to close her eyes, and she heard something like cannon fire. I thought who now is firing a cannon at this time of night? I looked up at mom, and she was asleep. So I laid back down, and I heard like old time music.

I'm talking like 1800's type of music. It sounded like it was coming out of an old 1920's radio, but really muffled sounding.

And then I got the taste of gun oil in my mouth. And then I could smell and taste really sweet lemons. I got up and said, to hell with this. I went back to the living room and turned on the television, and waited for the sun to come up. Just like a damn vampire, no sleep during the night, and sleep for an hour just after the sun rises. I'm surprised I don't have the fangs to go along with my problems.

The next morning I waited for mom to wake up. As usual Liz was already awake at the crack of dawn. No sleep for the wicked, as you say.

So finally when I woke up, Liz told me her story. I thought is was so cool, I couldn't wait to tell Connie and Johnny. But I asked Johnny what was it about the sweet smelling lemons? Johnny said, that back in the old days to sweeten their lemon aide, they would add lemon extract so that is how they would sweeten lemon aide. I would of just added sugar. But maybe sugar was hard to come by in those days.

HUGO, OK.

Hugo is a small almost forgotten town. Some of the biggest circuses used to come here for the winters. Then go back out on the road, come spring. The only thing that is left in Hugo, to remind us of this is the cemetery. And in one section of this is for circus performers only.

On the tombstones are their professions, and how they died. There is even an elephant and its beloved trainer buried together. Connie had been there, and she knew we would like to go to baby land.

We drove over to that section of the cemetery. Liz got out of the car, and walked down the sidewalk. I noticed that it was deadly quiet. There was no sound, no birds, no wind, not even the sound of people talking some distant from us.

Many of the headstones, there didn't even live until they were five years old. When we arrived back at Connie's house, we replayed the tape from the camcorder. It showed Liz walking down the sidewalk, and talking about how young the babies had died. But with each new grave, we heard creaking sounds. As if the coffin that was made from wood, was slowly opening to reveal the contents inside. No one said anything. There was a silence, that fell over the house. Like out at the cemetery that afternoon.

Until one of us said with hesitation, play that again. We listened to the tape again, and there on the tape was the same errie creaking noise that you only hear in those vampire movies. When the vampire is getting ready to exit his coffin, to feast on anyone who is wondering the night streets.

We played it again. And still couldn't believe what we were hearing. A few years later, Connie called us and asked if we could come to Texas for her younger daughter's wedding in June? And I thought why don't we go down in July for her birthday, and do a

21

baby shower for her oldest daughter. So we decided to go down each month. But before we got the tickets, Connie had called and said: " we are going to Jefferson, TX. I gota message saying we had to stay in the Jefferson Hotel, and that you guys were to stay in room 19. There you would get a message. Oh, by the way, it is the most haunted room in Jefferson. In the most haunted hotel in Jefferson."

I got on the phone and asked her:" are you freaking nuts?? Do you know how bad it is going to be for me and Liz?" Connie just said we had to stay in that hotel, and in that room. When we hung up with her, we both said we are going to kill her!! Well we had a few months to prepare ourselves for the next adventure in ghost hunting at its worse.

Jefferson, Texas

The town of Jefferson is reported to be the most haunted town in Texas. And the Jefferson Hotel is the most haunted hotel in Jefferson. So there we were in the most haunted hotel in Texas.

It was once a place for the ladies of the evening. And the reason I call them the ladies of the evening instead of prostitutes, is because of the way we were treated by them. But before the building was a hotel, it was a factory. But it was turned into a hotel, where the ladies would meet the gentlemen downstairs, and take them up to their bedrooms.

Before we start this story, you must be made aware of one fact: no employee of the hotel stays after5pm. No one is there to answer the switchboard, no one is there if you need help, no one will hear you scream, you are alone!! Remember the Haunting?

There is no desk clerk after 5pm, and they don't return until 8am. You will need to keep this in the back of your mind. No noe is in the hotel, execpt for the few guests that are staying in the hotel with you. The employees' leave right at 5pm, before it gets dark.

In room 19, the room is small and would normally take one maid to clean it. In this room, no maid will clean it alone. It takes two maids to the room.

Legend has it, that just after the warehouse was turned into a hotel. A young woman sat in room 19.

Her name has been lost over the years. But her story lives on. She was barely 18 years old, and her love for her young man ran deep through her soul. There was no one like him, he was tall with broad shoulders, black hair, and ice blue eyes. That melted when ever he saw her. She thought he loved her as much as she loved him. Both parents couldn't of been more happier. The date was set and in short of a week, they would be married in the new hotel.

The two was always together, it seemed like a fairy tale romance. When the day finally came, there in room 19 of the Jefferson Hotel sat the bride to be. With all of her friends around her fixing her hair, helping her to dress. It was almost time to be walked down the long beautiful staircase, where her father waited by the bottom of the staircase. To escort her to the preacher, where she expected her love of her life waited.

Then there was a knock on the door, there stood the bellboy with a note in his hand. She shooed all of her friends and family, out of the door. She took the note from the bellboy, and gentley smiled and a " thank you."

She slowly opened up the note, and started to read what was wrote. The note slowly floated to the floor. She walked over to the bed, and took the sheet from the bed and climbed upon the chair, and tied it around the chandler and then tied it around her neck and stepped off the chair.

The note was read aloud, for the people who had gathered for this joyous occation.

"Please forgive me, I don't love you and I don't want you as my wife." The young man was never seen or heard of again. The death of the young girl, remains.

We drove into town about 2pm, early enough to still have a clerk at the desk. The hotel looked like the mid 1800's. And as we walked into the place, it looked like the orginal furniture was there.

There was a deep red velvet couch. The couch color had looked like someone just bled all over it. On one side with a wood table in the center, and two yellow velvet arm chairs across from the faded red couch. On the walls were pictures of different people, and scenery.

There were displays cabinets, that held the desk log. Where people had signed during the late 1800's into the early 1900's. Some had old antiques in them. Above that hund down from the ceiling was a glass chandler.

We checked into the hotel, and was taking our bags up to our rooms. When I heard this young woman, I thought that she was by my side. Telling me how they had let the hotel go. And how these stairs were just terrible. And they needed to fix them, and to be careful on them. But when I turned to respond to her. There by my side was a young black girl, with a black dress and a white apron and a little white hat on. We were both on the same staircase. I turned to take the next few steps, and when I turned back, she was gone. A cold shiver went down my spine, if it wasn't for the fact that my car was sitting outside, I would drop my suitcase and run for it. I made my way down to our room, where Liz was already there waiting for me to come.

As we went to open the door, it felt like someone was on the other side of the door, holding it shut. But with a hard push, the door swung open. We put our suitcase on the only bed in the room, which was a double. A bit to small for two people. While I was in the room unpacking, Liz went out into the hallway and tried to call her dad. To tell him we had arrived safely. Liz couldn't get a hold of her dad.

And so we thought that we would try later to reach him. That maybe he was asleep. Liz looked at me and said, that she started not to feel very good. She started to get a real bad headache, and that she started to feel sick to her stomach.

We decided to go walk around the town, to see what we could see. Down the street about a block was another hotel, and across the street from that hotel was a train car. It belonged to Jay Gould. So we went inside, and looked around. We went back to the Excelsor Hotel, and we were going to sign up for their plantation breakfast. When we started to talk to the front desk clerk, about if the hotel was haunted? And she said that Jay Gould hauntes one of the rooms upstairs. And she began to tell us how one of Hollywood's directors was staying there with his film crew, and in the middle of the night he woke them and ledt the hotel room. Complaining that he was awaken by the ghost of Jay Gould, the 1929's millionaire. When we asked who the director was? She said, the one who made the ghost movies.

We then went and grabbed a bite to eat. The musuem was open, so we went through that also. We talked to one of the ladies about any haunting? And she told us, about the building that was straight down the street, that stood empty for years. And there was no power to it, but on certain nights you could see lights inside of it.

We then walked back to our hotel, and by then it was after 5pm. And the doors were locked up, which meant we had to us a number code to get inside the hotel.

No one was at the front desk. And then that old saying came to my mind: there is no one in the hotel, we are gone at 5pm, no one will hear you scream! I knew something was about to come, and it wasn't good. Connie pushed the code to the door, and it opened up. We went back upstairs,To our room 19. Where I left the door open. Liz tried to call her dad again, and there was still no answer. She started to get sicker.

A group of young adults was moving down the hall, and talking about how haunted room 19 was. By this time the group was coming down the hall towards room 19. Liz had come back into the room, and said a group of people wanted to see the room.

Now normally, I do not invite people into my house, let alone into a small room. Especially strangers. And here we are in a small town. There's no phone in my room, and no desk clerk ot answer it if we got into trouble.

But what do I do? I let them in, to see the most haunted room in the hote. One of the kids called, Shane. Started to tell us about the bathroom mirror. That if we turned on the hot water, and let the mirror get all steamed up. We would see a message on the mirror:" HELP, I'VE BEEN MURDERED!!" Well that was good enough for me. Liz went and turned on the hot water only, and closed the door.

As we waited for the mirror to steam up, Shane told us we would know when the mirror was ready. The pressure in the water would go down, and in few minutes after that we could go in and see the message. Those were the longest minutes in my life. Would there be a message? Was this the message me and Liz was supposed to get? Shane started to talk about the ghost walk they went on last night. Shane spoke up and said, I know where to go.

Liz spoke up and said, "it was time to open the bathroom door." Liz opened the door, and the way she did it was like a small child opening up a closet door. Done slowly as if a monster would jump out at her. And in that, I was thinking what kind of monster would jump out of the bathroom door.

As she opened it, she took pictures. The mirror was steamed up, Liz told everybody. But then she shut the door for some reason. Shane went and reopened the door, and the mirror was wiped clean. Liz was the only one to see the mirror, and the pictures she took to see the mirror was steamed up just a few seconds ago.

Liz went to turn off the hot water, to only discover the hot water was off. And the cold water on. Now how did the hot water turn off by its self, and the cold water turned on? Then she looked down, and noticed that there was water all over the floor. Like someone had a water fight in there.

When the pictures was developed, the floor had a gold glow to it. And when we saw the pictures of the mirror, one picture was of the fogged up mirror. And the next picture was of a woman in the mirror, made in the steamed up mirror. I thought I was going to die. But let us get back to the room. Shane took us through the town, to the ghost walk. We went by this old library, a few lights were on, and you were supposed to be able to see people inside of there. But we did not see anything.

But after we had our pictures developed, there was what might have been a mist in the library. We walked on and up to the next house. Which was an old plantation house. Where someone had gotten murdered. Well to our surprise as we walked up to the house, on the video camera, I started to get balls of light inside of the house.

And when you just looked at the house, that was no balls of light moving through the house. Then we started to hear a train's whistle, it was as if it was whistling from far away. And then as if it was being stretched out in the air, with an eerie sound toit. This went on for a few minutes.

We then went onto the next house. Liz decided not to come down, so I took all the cameras, while she stayed at the top of the hill. The rest of us went down to an empty field. Shane had started to tell thestory about the field. Long time ago, there was a house there and it belonged to captain, and his wife. When the captain was gone on his boat trips, his wife would have her lover come over. She would always look out the bedroom window, to watch for her husband to leave, and signal for her lover. That it was safe to come.

Well on one night she didn't watch for her husband to leave. She signaled for the lover.

The husband came back up the house, up to their room and had caught them together. It is said, that he killed them both. And buried the bodies on the property, and the house fell in on its self. No one knows how it happened. Since then no houses was built on the property.

I had taken a Polaroid pictures of where the house might have been. And when they developed, there was a house, and a lady of the house on watch for her husband. Meanwhile Liz was waiting at the top of the hill, and she was having her own experience. She could hear cannon fire goin on. It was as if we were in the middle of the Civil War. The ground trembled as if a thousand horsed was galloping by. Men screaming as if they had been injured. Bullets whistled through the air, and then stopped suddenly as if it had hit its mark, with a thud. We walked back up the hill, and I know Liz was getting a little sicker. And I had to admit that the thick of the night air was hard for us to breath. So we only had one more old building in town, that was just down the block from our hotel. We slowly made our way to the old building.

We ahd just been told that it used to be an old saloon, with the ladies of the evening on the top stairs. So we took pictures, and me and Liz leftthe group and headed for the hotel.

We used the code on the door, and entered the quite hotel. We sat in the lobby, and waited for the others to come back. We had tried and experiment in our room earlier, during the day. We had left the room with a tape recoreder, going to see if we could pick up any noises. But we had forgotten about our experiment until we returned to the hotel. Connie and Shane came through the door, and told us of how Shane had taken them down to a place. In the field, was a square piece of wood. That was about a foot off the ground, where they sold slaves. And it was called a slave block. How awful that must have been. Having families torn apart for the sakes of slavery. We went back up to our room.

We sat on our bed for a few minutes, and talked about the evenings events. When we noticed the forgottentape recorder. We rewind the tape and started to listen. We heard the door shut. And then the voices started to laugh and talk. We couldn't understand what was being said. But it sounded like it was good time. Then we started to hear what sounded like furniture being moved. But when we had entered the room, nothing was amiss.

When we started to notice the chandler started to move, it swung back and forth. We got a few pictures of it moving. And it just stopped just as abrupt as it started. We turned on the television, and Cleopatra had just started. So we turned up the volume, and tried to get some sleep. Since we were the only ones at the end of the hallway. I had decided not to get undressed, Liz just took off her pants.

We had just laid back on the bed, when I heard this soft tapping on the wall outside. And just as I asked Liz if she had heard it? A strong smell of smoke came into the room. And it wasn't just any kind of smoke, but the worst smoke, it was cigar smoke.

We both tried not to think of what it was, or who would be smoking in a smoke free hotel. When I looked over towards Liz, and there in the old rocking chair was a man. Dressed in black, with a gold watch chain hooked to the buttons of his vest, and a black cowboy hat. He had a mustache, and when he smiled it showed his dimpled cheeks. He was puffin on a small cigar. And when he noticed that I was looking at him, he smiled with:" HELLO, DARLING!!" Then he disappeared leaving on the smell of cigar smoke left in the room.

I was finally able to lift my hand to shake Liz, with a shaky voice:" cigar man." With that we both decided it was time to close our eyes and sleep. We didn't dare talk about what I had seen. About two hours into our sleep, I thought Liz had pulled all the blankets off of me. And so I pulled them back over onto me and fell back to sleep. When a knock came to the door. We both woke and said:" GHOSTS!!" When the knock came again, and I said with a shaky voice:" Connie?" And a man's voice came back and said no, Shane.

I jumped out of bed, and went over to answer the door. I had forgotten that Liz wasn't fully dressed. At that time and when I opened the door to see Shane, standing outside of our door. The first words out of his mouth was there is an emergency at your house. And there was a cop waiting for you down stairs. As we walked down the hallway to the stairs, I started to talk to Liz who I thought was next to me. As mom was thinking she was talking to me, I was getting on my pants on. And running down the hallway to my aunt Connie's room. To tell her that my dad had a heart attack.

Now before I knew the whole truth, mom never came back up to tell me about dad. She just got down the stairs to talk to the cop.

Now back to where my mom was talking to me. I was just asking her what it could be? Maybe my mother had finally died. But who would know where to reach us? We came to the stairs, where I turned again to talk to Liz, and she wasn't there. Then I realized she wasn't with us in the hallway.

Liz had no time to put her pants on, when me and Shane left the room. So just who or what walked with us down that hallway? And why did I think it was Liz? We got down to the front desk, and there in the lobby stood a policeman, waiting to tell me the information.

Then all of the sudden Liz and Connie came running down the stairs. And how did Liz know to go and get Connie? Liz came and stood next to me and the officer was telling us, that Ray had a heart attack. And he gave us the number to the hospital, and that Krissy had been trying to get a hold of us. The officer turned and left. I tried to call the hospital, but the doctor was busy. And would call us back. As we all sat there. Me, Liz Connie, Shane, and his wife. Shane began to tell us what happened to them.

They had been awakened by the phone in their room. Ringing and when they picked it up to answer it, no one was there. It kind of scared them. So they came out to the lobby to sit for a few minutes. When the officer knocked on the door. Shane said that he let him in, and the cop told him to go up to where Elizabeth and Darlene Gould was. Staying in room19, and get them for me. I interrupted him at this point, and I said:" why didn't he just come up and get us?" And Shane said: "the cop didn't ask? He told me to go up and get you." We talked to the doctor, and Ray was stable. So we all went back up stairs to try and get some sleep. Now we need to rewind these events. To when we were getting ready to go on our ghost hunt.

Liz was sick, saying that she did not want to go on the ghost tour. At that time, Ray was having chest pains, and was not feeling good.

Now Texas and Arizona are two hour different times. And at that time, Liz was trying to get a hold of her dad.

By the time we were back at the hotel, and getting ready for bed. It was 9pm at home. And Liz had tried again for her dad, with no answer. I told her we would try again in the morning. But Liz still had this sickness. That would not go away, and she started to have this bad feeling that something was wrong. Meanwhile back homw, dad had gone to the hospital, with his heart attack. Our good friend, Krissy was at her mother's house with her two kids. All of the sudden she got the feeling to go home.

She told her mom that she would be right back. That she had to go home and check her messages. One of the messages told her that Ray was in the hospital. And that she needed to get a hold of us now. So she called her mom, and said that she won't be home forawhile.

She went over to the Virgin River. Where me and Liz works, and told the operators to try and find us. We were asleep. And that was about two hours later.

Meanwhile Krissy went to the hospital to check on Ray. He was not doing good, when she got there. She heard a nurse say: " his blood pressure was dropping, and then threre was a yell, his heart had stopped." When she saw us, how could she tell us that he died. So all she could do was to pray, and pray, and cry. The doctor came out and asked Krissy, " where is his family?" She told him that we were in Texas. He said, "if you want to see him, he is now stable." She smelled a very strong odor of coffee. Just like it was brewed fresh. She looked outside the room to see if anyone was drinking coffee, and no one had coffee.

So she went and called her dad to come to the hospital, with another one of her friend's dad. He was a bishop, to give dad a blessing. So now we are back in Jefferson, and we are just getting into bed, when my mom noticed the television's volume was down. She asked me if I turned it down? And I said, I didn't touch it. So we climbed into bed, and fell asleep until day break.

We got up and started to pack our bags, so that we could be ready when Connie and Johnny met us downstairs.

As we closed the door, a small voice said:" we are so sorry to hear about your husband." At that time I looked atLiz, and I looked at the door. Across from us the door lock chain started to swing against the wood of the door, causing a scraping sound. We both looked at each other, and Liz said:" don't run, mom."

That was the only thing that stopped me from running down the hall to the staircase. As we started to discuss the evening's events again. We did receive the message, if I didn't tell Liz to let Shane into see the room. He never would of met us. And why wouldn't the cop come up the stairs to room 19? Was he to scared to come into the hotel any further then the front desk?

The biggest question at this point was, who put the call threw to Shane's room? Remember there is no one here after 5pm, to transfer the phone call for the switchboard. So who put the call threw to Shane's room? We caught the next flight out of Dallas to Las Vegas. Where we called Krissy Thornton. She started to tell us what happened. That there was a strange smell of coffee, just in Ray's room. We told her it was Ray's mom, she loved coffee with a passion. So when ever she comes around, her smell to us is her coffee just being made fresh.

She took us to dinner, and told us how she had to leave her kids at her mom's house. And that she just had to get home to get this message, hat was waiting for her. Krissy is a sort of person, would never leave her kids behind.

It it wasn't and emergency, or some other real good reason. And because the day she got her message, was on a Sunday. And everybody who knows Krissy, knows she spends Sunday dinne with her parents. So she told us she got him a blessing, and put his name in the Temple for prayer. The events that happened in Jefferson, can can not be explained. It had been two years since, that night and we still go over on how we were there at that time.

And why Shane's phone rang. And how Krissy knew to go home at that time, and how she smelled coffee in the ICU ward. Could that have been Henrietta or somebody else?

I don't think so, only Henrietta would come with that smell. To come and help Ray out, who knows? Maybe one day it will be explained. Until then we still wonder how and the whys, this happened in three different states at the same time.

LAS VEGAS

The lights of Las Vagas has not even shown for even one hundred years. But even so, the ghosts are still there. In what they call old Vegas. The area around the Freemont Street where the first casino's once stood tall, and the hot desert floor was the Flamingo, The Horseshoe, not to mention the rest. But it is the Horseshoe that we are going to visit.

We always valet park. Anyone who knows the heat of Vegas in the summer does the same. Its just to hot to walk. We had decided to go to the Horseshoe Casino.

As we walked threw the doors, there were still the red carpet and the crystal chandliers, the sound of the slot machines with the coins dropping into the coin tray. And then something happened.

The faded red carpet wasn'tfaded anymore, ladies in long evening gowns with their white gloves, men in tuxes, the crystal chandliers hung from the ceilings with the lights that twinkled. Jackpots in the one arm bandits going off all over the casino. People screaming with joy at winning. Men with bulging chests walking through the crowds. This was Vegas. This is also the time when you could disappear into one of the lots in the desert only to be forgotten.

As we wondered through the casino, and watched the people gambling and the fun that was ine the air. In order to get to your car, the valet was at the top of the casino. So we started to walk towards the valet parking. As we left the gambling area behind, we also left the noise behind.

Me and Liz was behind Ray, and we were talking and laughing about the different things that had happened during the day. We had turned down this long hallway, and there wasno way out except forward. Or to turn around and go back the way we had just come.

When we felt like we were being followed. I turned my head around just so I could get a peak of who was following us. When I caught out the corner of my eye, a man in a black tux was following us. I grabbed onto Liz, and asked her to look behind us. And she did. Our speed picked up, as we hurried towards the valet parking area. I looked over at Liz, and I knew she had seen what I had, and she was thinking what I was. When we had finally reached the valet, Ray turned to us and asked us, what was the hurry? And we both turned to look for the two men that was following us, and there was no one. We were the only ones that was at the valet. The men in the tuxes were gone, and so was the feeling of being followed.

When the valet person returned with the car, I asked about the two men? He told us that a few people have asked him the same question. And this what he told us.

"Back in the fifties when Vegas was new, there were men or more flatly called the mob. And they used this area to walk people to the cars that took them away, never to be seen again. There was a gun battle up here, and several of the men in tuxes were killed up here."

Where the men that followed us the ghosts of those men who was killed? We will never know. But is what we do know, is that people who valet cars at the Horseshoe. And walk to the valet parking area, are followed by two men dressed in black tuxes. And they have noticeable bulge in the jackets where maybe a gun lies in wait.

Just miles South of Vegas, and just before the California border, lies three casinos the one we are about to talk about is the Prim Valley Resort. The famous bank robbers in history's car lay's in state. In a glass tomb, is the car of Bonnie and Clyde. And you might ask why is this so worthy a story? Has any of the people who ghost hunt ever found the ghost of Bonnie and Clyde? Who would think in this small town that only hosts casinos, would be the resting or none resting place of the famous duo. But there are so many miles from where they died, is the car hat they lost their lives in. We took pictures of the famous car. And when they came out.

There in the car, is an image of a girl who looks like Bonnie. And on the outside of the car leaning against the front end of the car is Clyde, with his gun. And he is in the shirt that he wore the day he lost his life.

There are no pictures that show him in that shirt. But there he is, in the same shirt and he is just standing there. We took pictures of the side of the car, and it looks as if lights are coming out of the car.

And if you dare slip your hand between the glass partitions, there is a breeze that's in the glass. But also notice how the air outside the glass is not moving. May be we have found the ghosts of Bonnie and Clyde, who knows? Judge for yourself.

SAN DIEGO GHOST TOURS

We have visited San Diego Ghost tours several times, and what we are about to tell you, are what we saw there. We went into the Whaley House, several times and each and every time we experienced new and better things.

Our first time on the ghost tours, we met at a hotel down town San Diego. As our tourguide was talking about the hotel and how it was haunted, Liz turned around to me and accused me of pulling on her back pack. And I told her, " I had done no such thing." When she was pulled on it again. At that point I started to take pictures of the back of Liz. What developed in the pictures was a large streek across the picture.

With each house we entered, we could feel that the house felt as if we were not alone.

In the William Morse House, the guide was talking about this one room, that had a small child's bed in it. And he explained how two injured soldier's had slept in the bed.

We took some pictures of the bed, and when they were developed that on the bed was, the white streak going over the bed. And then we took a picture of the staircase, and there on the stairs was the same white streak. We went to the San Diego's graveyard, which is the oldest part of San Diego. It is the oldest graveyard in San Diego.

The guide talked about many people, who had lost their lives in the early days of San Diego. When the city digged up the graves, they took all the grave stones. But left the bodies! So now who ever parks their car on the street, their horns go off. They come out in the morning to start their cars, and it has a dead battery. And the apartment buildings that they built, over the graves they all have strange things happen to them.

We took pictures of the grave yard and needless to say, there was what looked like ground fog in the grave yard. And there was no ground fog that night. The fog came out in the pictures, but not the video camcorder.

Then when the pictures was laid next to each other, we discovered that along the fence line we had what appeared to be moving lights. It reminded me of the scene in the Poltergeist movie, where the spirits came down the stairs in the house. We went down the road from there into the Whaley House.

When we entered the Whaley House, there was a caretaker of the house. That let us in, she was dressed in normal dress, and told us about the house. Me and Liz started to walk around the house, taking pictures of the house.

Liz came around the stairs and when she looked up, at the stairs there was this woman dressed in black. With her hair tied back in a bun, and it looked as if she hasn't washed in at least a week.

She told Liz, that she was sorry that she scared her. But she was not expecting guests. But it was nice to have people there.

The caretaker reappeared and told Liz, that in the kitchen area, some of the people had caught ghosts on pictures. So into the kitchen, Liz went to take some pictures.

Meanwhile the tour guide directed us all into the courtroom, that is part of the Whaley House.

So Liz was taking pictures in the kitchen area, the woman dressed in black came, up to Liz and told her that she needed to go to the courtroom. Where the other people had been assembled.

So Liz came into the courtroom. The tour guide had asked us all to take a seat, so he could tell us about Mr. Whaley and the house. Well we went to sit down on the chairs thatwas next to us.

The chair creaked like someone had just sat on it. Me and Liz started at each other. Then we looked around and there standing next to me was the woman in black.

And we talked about the pictures on the wall, and other stuff. And then it was time for us to leave the house, the caretaker went over to open the double doors to the outside and they refused to budge.

After a few minutes of tugging on the doors, they finally released and opened. As we left the house, we asked the caretaker, who was theother lady in the period dress? The one in the black dress? She looked at us, and said:" what lady?" On the way back on the bus, we asked if anyone else saw her? And no one else saw the woman in black.

Liz commented on how she said, she was sorry if she scared her but she wasn't expecting guests. The fact was we were on a tour. We were expected. The next time we went to the Whaley House, we were on a tour again. Only my sister Connie was with us. This time we went to the Whaley House during the day.

It was during the time of day that all of the kids were in school. We went through the house, and the people told us that they had some experiences during the day, and with the curtains moving and so forth.

So Liz took some pictures and we just wondered around and left. We came back that night on the tour that we had taken, two years before. And we went back to all the same places as we did before, and then we came to the Whaley House. And it came time for us to go into the courtroom, and me an Liz and another lady, from the tour was talking in the dinning room.

And we were talking about our camera's going in and out of focus. And Liz started to go around the table. And into the kitchen area, when the part of the table she had walked away from, only seconds ago the chair fell. Wrapping itself around the leg of the table. But when it fell the sound on the hardwood floor, sounded as if a chest had fallen over.

The chair was so fragile, that if you just looked at it wrong, it would fall apart. But the noise rang through the house.

The caretaker came running into the dinning room, and we said it at once: " we didn't do it." The chair just fell over.

When we joinded the others in the courtroom, they all turned and looked at us, and we said we didn't to anything. It just fell over. The noise of it was so loud, that everyone in the courtroom heard it above the noise of everyone talking.

When we returned home, and had the pictures of a child, who was black and had a cloth tied around her head like a turban, it looked like a slave of the 1800's. She was just standing outside of the house. The third time we went to the Whaley House, we took Ray, my husband.

We left him in the courtroom to rest. We went around and filmed and took pictures. We went upstairs, and there in a sealed off bedroom with glass. The curtains were moving as if someone had opened a window, to allow the fresh air. We showed several people of the curtains moving, we also caught on film.

We went back to the hotel room, and looked at the film that we had taken. And while Liz was filming just outside of the courtroom, Mrs. Whaley walked through the pictures and outside of the building.

We never seen her while we were filming, but there she is on our disk. Just walking through the area, just as if there was nothing going on.

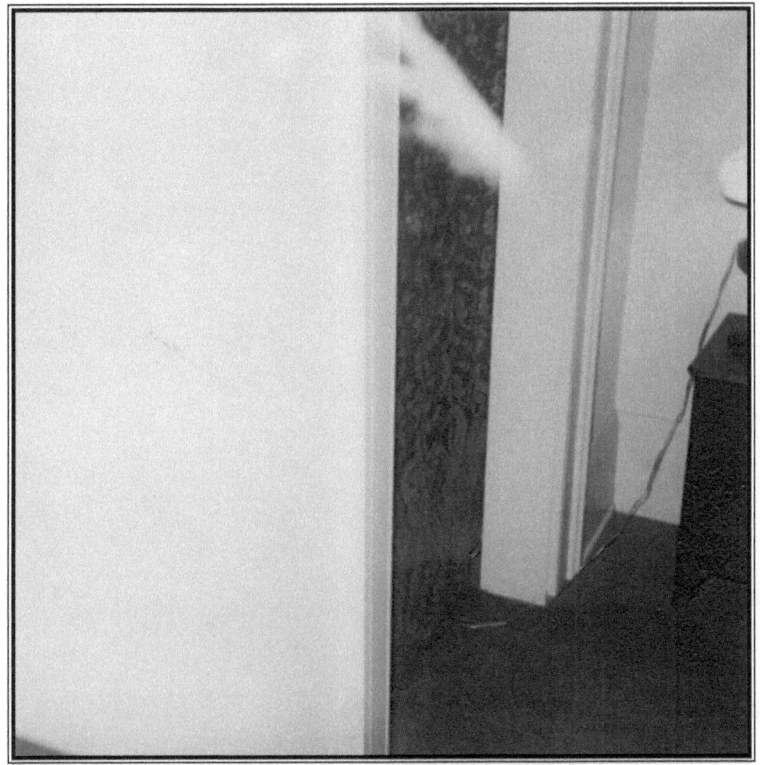

We have not been back to the Whaley House, but it seemed that every time we visit, the place we get more of the haunting that goes on in that old home.

GRAFTON, UTAH

Grafton, Utah is a small town. If you could call it a town.

In the 1800's pioneers settled the area, either floods or the attack of Indians took its toll on the settlement. But what made Grafton famous, was a film in the 1970's called Butch Cassidy and the Sundance Kid. It is the movie where Paul Newman rides the bike.

Well I knew of the town, because I lived in St. George during the time they were filming the movie. So I decided to take the family on a side trip one day, and we went to Grafton.

The settlement is fenced in and out in the middle of nowhere. Its hard to find, there is no signs to point the way. We saw the cemetery and decided to stop on the way out.

Some of the buildings are about to fall in on themselves. The ones that are still standing, we went over to look in the first one was the courthouse.

We had to look in through the windows the sun is high in the sky. The mountains can only be seen if you walk around the small one room building. So I put the camera up against the window, and I snapped away. We started to go to the next building, and both me and Liz started to hear music. Someone was playing a violin, and the closer we got we could hear people starting to talk. Then as we got up along the side of the building, everything stopped.

And is all we could hear was the whistling of the wind. We only had our camera. And the more we walked around the old buildings the quieter it got.

We started to get ready to go, and decided to go up to the cemetery. We got out of the car, and started to read the grave stones. Most of the people there had died in Indian raids.

While some died in a flood that had hit one spring. Liz was taking pictures of the graves, when she heard a voice say to her:" and what is that?"

We always thought that the voice was talking about the camera. We have not went back to see if we could hear the music or the voice.

Queen Mary

The Queen Mary, one of the last of the great luxury liners that is still left, over from an age that has long gone from us.

It now stands as part hotel, part museum. In Long Beach, California. This great ship still offers us the thrills, if we are game enough to just listen. On our first trip to the Queen Mary, we went on the tour. Meanwhile Ray was left on the deck to wait for us. We were just a few minutes late in getting to the room, where the guide was discussing the past events of the Queen Mary.

The room was dark, except for the television monitors that was left on. But as I was looking around the room, I noticed a woman in a pale yellow dress that looked like it had an empire waist. It was long enough to reach the floor. As I watched her, she only lingered for only a few minutes or so.

She started to walk to a part of the wall which I thought was a door, because she walked though it.

A moment later the lights came on, and I had forgotten about the woman, and started to follow the rest of the group out the door. It won't be until the next visit that we talk about the lady in the yellow dress. We went into the bowels of the ship. As we were going to the engine room, me and Liz was separated only a few feet.

I looked around for Liz, and she was not behind me. So I went to look for her, and she came at a fast walk to me and said:" couldn't you hear me scream for you?" And I said, "no." " I just came to find you, you wasn't behind me."

Liz started to tell me, that she had many arms surrounding her. And that they trapped her in a corner, and would not let her go. And at that time she was screaming for help. Liz was only ten feet away, from the group and not one of us heard her scream for help.

Some unknown force had held her in a corner, and some how muffled her voice, so no one could hear her scream.

We caught up with the rest of the group, and stopped the elevator from leaving us. And the guide was talking about the man that had been killed. The door that shut tight to keep out the water. There at the door, was the young man who had been killed. And for a moment, then he disappeared. The tour came to an end, and we had taken lots of phots and then we were told we could wonder around the ship if we wanted to. Me and Liz decided to wonder around the ship. We came to these beautiful wood staircases.

When Liz started to vision the woman, who was coming down the staircases to the men who were waiting for them to take them to dinner. As Liz was talking about this. I was filming on our camcorder. And to our shock on the film it shows a woman's hand, coming down onto the banister. Very gracefully with her long manicured fingers, placing them on the railing.

Then we see her brown dress, starting to cover Liz's blue pants. But not being able to see this while I was filming, I moved away from Liz.

We found our way back up to the upper decks of the ship. There waiting for us was Ray. He asked how the tour went? And we told him about it, and we started to wallk away when Ray started to tell us about the the captain of the ship. And how he just walked away from him, not even saying anything at all to him. And when I asked him how he knewit was the captain of the ship? He said he had on a captain's uniform.

We walked down the deck of the ship. Where there was some pictures of the ship dating back in the forties. Ray stood there and pointed to the one picture that had a captain in it, that's the one who just passed me by. As we looked closer at the picture. The captain on the picture said:" the last captain's of the Queen Mary." We both turned to Ray, and said: you've seen a ghost!"A year later we took my sister on the Queen Mary.

As we drove up onto the tar mat of the parking lot of the Queen Mary. As me and Liz stepped out of the car, on the tar mat we heard a voice that said:" WELCOME BACK, WE ARE GLAD TO SEE THAT YOU'VE RETURNED!!"

I looked up at the ship, and saw a sailor in a deep blue wool coat, that button down the front. He also had on a officer's cap. And then he was gone. And I was starting to get sick. Liz was already on her way to the bathroom.

I soon followed her. Connie and I went on the tour. And once again I found myself in the same room, where the presitation would take place. The room was well lit, and so I looked for the door that the woman in the yellow dress went through just a year earlier. But to my horror, the wall was solid. There was no door, in which she could just simply walk out of.

The only thing I could think of was, she went through the wall as easily as we cross the room. One of the host's was in the room, so I went over to them and asked if they had anyone that took on the role of a ghost? During the presentation abouta year ago? I was told that they did not need to do that. That they have enough ghosts on board.

I then told them about the woman in yellow. And he said," she's one of our ghosts." Then almost like an after thought, he asked:" did you get it on tape or picture by any chance?" I said, "no."

We went through the ship, and nothing that wecould detect happened. It was only after we got back home, and we had our pictures developed. That we found what we did not see with our eyes but the eyes of the camera caught.

While we were going through the World War II display. We were at the hospital part of the ship, and we were taking pictures of the rooms. Were the injured would be, as a curtain that divided the two beds. Against the one curtain is a soldier that is dressed like a marine.

You can see the legs and the boots, and the white beltthat goes around the waist. The rest is invisible.

The next picture is of a window display of the toys, that the children played with while they were on the Queen Mary. The window display is about three by three feet. But the picture, looks like it is ina room.

In the room is the toys and a old school desk, and on the desk is a woman and a small child. Thewoman is slightly bent over the small child. I need to back up, and take a back a statement. Something did happen the last time we were on the Queen Mary. Me and Connie had to seek out a bathroom, and Liz didn't need to go. So while we were in the bathroom, she went down the hall.

And when we came out of the bathroom, she coming up the hall. We could tell something was wrong. She was shivering as if she had come out of a meat locker. Her lips were almost blue. And she could hardly talk from shaking so much.

We asked her what was wrong? She finally got the words out. " Theres a little girl hanging onto me!" That is what prompts us to take the picture of the display case. The pictures of the soldier and the display, are Polaroid pictures. So they can not be tampered with.

The last time we visited the Queen Mary, it was just me, Liz, and Ray. We went to retake pictures of the ones we had, but when we went to the World War II area it was gone.

It was something else. I so wanted to see the area where someone was taking a picture of me, while I was taking a picture of them. To see if it was real or not. In the picture there is this old camera. With hands in gloves that is holding this camera, that looks to be in the 1930's or older. With only these gloved hands holding it up, when I had taken a picture with my camera. But the area was being readied to hold something else. So we went up to the other the end of the ship.

Up there was the ballroom, and some restaurant, and of course they didn't open up until later. But we decided to go into the restaurant any way. I was filming on the dvd camcorder, and Liz was taking pictures.

But as we entered the restaurant, we could hear the dishes clinking as if they were being gathered up from the table.

A faint sound of music was in the air. And then we started to pick up whispering. As if the place was full of customers. But we knew they weren't. We sat and discussed it and then we left.

We went to go past the ballroom, when we could hear dance music coming from inside. So we peaked into see if there was anyone there. And there on the dance floor wasa lone dancer.

Slowly dancing to the music, until she stopped, and was staring at us for only a few seconds. Then she was gone, and so was the music.

If we could of, we would screamed and run. But as a reminder from Liz, mom don't run they can catch you. That was the last time we visited the Queen Mary.

MOUNTAIN MEADOW MASSACRE

Mountain Meadow Massacre happened back in the 1840's, when Utah was being settled. And the murder of the many church members.

The way to the west coast ran threw Cedar City, in southern Utah. It was this one wagon train that was on its way to California, and all the riches that drew the people to the coast.

In Mountain Meadow, the wagon train made camp for a couple of days. To let the stock feed and rest.

The rest of the true story died with the people on the wagon train. No one knows why the members of the church, and the local tribe of Indians attacked the party of the wagon train.

They killed everybody above the age of eight years old. The young children, was after a period of time returned to their relatives living in the east.

There is two monuments, there is one on a hill over looking the valley. And the other is in the valley, on the spot they think that the pioneers buried their victums. We went there around the anniversary date of the killings. We sat on the benches, and listened to the calm of the valley.

That is until I heard the first swish of an arrow, and what sounded like a thing hitting something hard. Then I heard it again. And again, and again. I then heard a scream. I turned to see who it was screaming, and found that no one else was bothered by what I had heard.

Is what I was hearing, from the past? The massacre was going on again! Is all I could hear was screaming by the woman, and sounds of arrows passing me by in the air.

Then came the whistling of the bullets, and that horris sound as it makes contact with something solid. The groans of men being cut down, where they stood. Children's cries of help. And the cries of pain. I couldn't get out of the events going on around me. Then Liz came up and put her hand on my shoulder, "mom," and she shook me and finally yelled:" MOM!" I finally came around and wiped the tears from my face. I waited a while, before I asked her if she felt that?

The pain that is still in the meadow, is still grim reminder of the injustice that was done there over one hundred and forty years ago.

We decided togo up to the upper monument. But as we crossed over the small creek, something told me to take pictures of the group of trees, that is growing in the bank of the creek.

We got into our car and drove up the hill, that overlooked the valley. And on top of the hill, is the monument of all of the people who died there. There is also the names of the children, that survived the attack.

We sat and looked out over the valley, and while we sat still. The sound of little feet shuffling along the area, as if some of the children was up there and walking around us. We had our camcorder on and just recording the valley, and the mountains surrounding the area. When we got home, the sounds was on the tape. The sounds of something walking on the rocks, and when I got the pictures developed there in the trees was a man, and a woman standing together in periond dress of the 1800's.

THIS IS THE PLACE MONUMENT

This is the Place Monument is located next to the Hogal Zoo, in Salt Lake City, Utah. It is a state park, and has a large monument to the pioneers who helped settled the Salt Lake Valley. Or some of the pioneers.

Up the hill is a pioneer village, that has all the old buildings that has been gathered from all over the state. We went into several of the buildings, and saw how they conducted their business of the day. But we came to a school house, that had been transported to the village.

In this old school building was the period chairs, and desks of time. There was no traffic on the outside of the old school house. But yet the windows started to shake as if there was a large dump truck had just went by. As luck would have it, I was on the new video camcorder. And hadn't learned how to operate it just yet. I thought that I had turned it on, when we fould out it wasn't recording. What we had missed is the following.

We heard the windows shake, and decided to try to talk to the spirits if there was any. Liz started out saying: " if there is anyone who would like to talk to us, please tap once for yes, and twice for no." Well nothing happened.

Then I remembered that this was an old school house, that inhabited young children of a time that they could of died from a cold.

So I started to sing an old church song. On Ward Christian Soldiers. And I hadn't gotten through the first line, when we started to hear knocking on the window pane.

Meanwhile Liz was taking pictures inside of the small one room school house. The more questions I asked, the more knocking came.

I went over to the windows to make sure that no one out there, to do the window knocking.

There was no one out there. I then went to the other side of the room, and looked outside of the windows. And there was no one there.

We were competley alone. So I started up the questions again. One question was, did you die in this room? The knock came back as a yes. It was a eight year old boy. And he loved going to school. We spent about an hour listening to the knocking on the window seal. We didn't want to leave, but we had to go. We never went back. We got the pictures developed, and the orbs that was in all of the pictures, was unbelievable.

MIDWAY AIRCRAFT CARRIER

Once when we were in San Diego, California. We took the wrong turn and ended up at the docks where the Aircraft Carrier Midway was docked.

So me and Liz thought that it would be great fun to go on the ship. Little did we know that with out so called gifts, we were just asking for it.

We paid the entry fee, to go on board and look around. The moment we stepped foot on the deck it should of told us, but did we listen? Oh, no that would be he ones who never get into trouble. So off we went. We started down the first hallway or corridor, as they say. And before we could even step over the step of where the door shuts tight. The pipe up above us started to move. We started the camcorder up and got it on tape.

And I went to go through the door way, when a burst of air pushed me back against the wall. Something had just came down the stairs. And so we decided to move along the way.

All the way we could smell bured tires and flesh. And it started to get really bad when we reentered the main area, of where we had come in at. Liz said that she needed some milk, that she was feeling kind of sick. So I sat her down on the bench, and went to find her some milk at the snack bar just around the corner of where she was sitting.

I found her some milk, and I started to feel sick myself. So I got myself some milk too. All the while the odor of the burned tires and human flesh was becoming over whelming.

I made it back to Liz and gave her the milk, and sat down beside her to drink mine. Her first words out of her mouth was, " You are never going to believe what just happened to me!!" "Okay, I just said tell me."

" I was just sitting here minding my own business, when out of the blur came this voice up to me and said: " GET THE HELL UP, AND OFF YOUR LAZY ASS. AND HELP GET THIS FIRE OUT!!" I looked around to see who was talking to me, and didn't see anyone when the voice told me again, to get off my lazy ass, and help put out this fire.

Well I told him, that there was no fire, and that he was dead. And that's when you walked up and it was gone." " Well did you get up off your lazy ass and help put out the fire?" It was all I could do was not laugh at poor Liz, and her ghost.

When ever I think about it, it still makes me laugh. But that's why we could smell the burned tires and flesh. We went outside, and went up on the top of the flight deck. We couldn't stay long up there, they were setting up for some party. But what we did feel was not good.

Lots of death and just not Americans either. The screaming of the engines as they suddenly exploded, and the ship moved from the force. We went over to some of the planes that was on top of the flight deck, and listened to the wind slowly blow in and around the planes. Men running so fast that they appeared to be nothing more than a blur in the open air.

Voices shouting out commands. The stench of burning tires, and human flesh once again inflamed our noses.

We stood there coughing trying to force the stench from our lungs. And then it was gone. The planes that was on fire, the men running around the deck, the stench from the air.

We could breath once again. We left the ship to its ghosts, and the air that seemed to engulf you of what happened there so long ago.

DISNEYLAND

We had been to Disneyland several different times, but it was on this time that we were to visit the park that we would experience.

What no one else in the park could never noticed. It had been a long day of doing the rides, and meeting with Krissy, Preston, and her two girls. Emerald and Burgandy. Me and Liz was just worn out.

So we decided that we would go into the halls of Presidents, and watch the show sitting down. And Krissy decided to go on more rides. So there sat me and Liz, to watch the show.

We didn't know that they had changed the show to a video of the first fifty years. We missed almost of what Steve Martin had to say.

We sat down in our seats, and waited for the lights to go down. While we were waiting, it was as if something had came up and sat down beside us, and took a seat. But that couldn't of been, because me and Liz was sitting next to each other.

The feeling that was with this person who sat next to us, was so calm and nice as if he had never done nothing wrong in his life. We both experienced the same thing at the same time. The person began to speak. And we both heard him.

The voice was soft and gentle. And this is what he said:" I am so proud of this place. The way it has grown. The way that my employee's had treated the people who come here to have fun, and escape the worries that their world has to offer them. I am just so proud of howthis, my dream has turned out.

Ladies enjoy this place of wonderment, and come back and visit me." Then there was a soft laugh. And the area between me and Liz, slid back intoplace. And he was gone.

But it left tears in our eyes. And eh feeling that we had met, someone who truly loved Disneyland, as much as we did. Whether or not, it was Walt Disney or not. We felt it was. And the pride he felt in his parks, his workers, and they joy that he had brought so many people was totally unreal. We both feel that we were both so tired, and our minds so relaxed.

That it was no hard for that spirit to enter our minds and talk to us, knowing that we would hear him. And maybe get hismessage out to the workers, in the different parks of just how proud he was of them.

We will never forget that day. And we will look up it as one of our favorite times.

KANAB, UTAH

Kanab, Utah is the place where all the westerns were shot, with the fantastic views of the red rock cliffs and monuments. It was the favorite place for John Wayne, and all of the western actors since.

There in Kanab, is a place called the movie set. It is just outside of town, and it has movie sets on it. And in their main restaurant it has old pictures of movie stars.

And there isa gift shop, out in front as you walk in. We went out back to where the movie sets were, and its in a big circle. There is a jail, and other different places. Like a barber shop, and a rooming house, and just different things like this.

We started out walking around the sets and going into some of the sets. Some of the sets we took pictures. And in the jail was this old boot in the cell. We laughed about it and Liz took a picture of it just for fun. We next saw this one movie set, with mirrors in it.

And it looked really strange. And it was almost like some one was looking back at you. But you just couldn't put your finger on what it was. We moved around the circle and came upon a sweat lodge. And it was just that, a sweat lodge. We moved around to where it looked like some rooming house was, but found out that it was just a painting on wood boards and nothing more.

Liz took a picture of it, and we went into the main restaurant. And was looking at some of the pictures of the movie stars.

Liz started to take pictures, of the old stars. She took John Wayne, Clark Gable, and Carol Lombard, and few of the other stars. And we left. But when we got home, and got our pictures developed. There across the faces of John Wayne, he pictures ofClark Gable, and Carol Lombard, white slashed that went across the pictures.

And then noticed that where the boot was in the jail house, was orbs. We then looked at the paintings of the rooming house, that was painted on the wood fence.

And there in the window was a woman standing in the window with the drapes pulled back, and she looked like a dance hall girl of the 1800's.

We made plans to go back, up there and ask questions, of the lady of the gift shop. With in two weeks we were back up there. And we went out to the paintings on the wall. There was no painting of a saloon girl in the window, the draps were painted shut. We went back into the restaurant to the pictures. None of the pictures had the light, coming from the outside, to create such a light.

We next went to the lady, who ran the gift shop. And asked her if she had other people ask about the pictures turning out funny? She did once see something float across the back lawn, asn disappear into the mist one morning. We left Kanab, and haven't been back to the movie sets. There is the place where time does stand still, for at least some of us.

SILVER REEF

Silver Reef is located between St. George and Cedar City, on I-15 in Utah. Silver Reef is only two of the known places in the world which they have silver in the sand stone.

The town was booming in the 1850's. Anything and everything went on. There are only two buildings left open, to the public. Its part gallery and part museum.

As we got out of our car, I was met by a miner. He was medium height, and he had a full beard, and wore a hat. And he was dusty, as if he had just come from the mine, and was on his way home.

He was a little bit nervouse, and then he was gone. Me and Liz walked into the building, and there was a young lady, who greeted us. And told us to look around.

But before she left us, she turned and said: " we can't get that part of the building warm." And pointed towards the museum part of the building. And it was no wonder, she had a little girl. Who was wondering around that part of the building.

As I was looking at the pictures of the town's people, there she was. Standing just as pretty as you please. Inside of the photo of the town's people, who lived over one hundred years ago.

We went over to where there was a safe, inside of the building. With every picture we took inside of the vault, a strange blue light appeared on the wall.

We went into the back of the bank, and there in the back was just sitting on one or the display cases, was a picture of a miner. That had appeared to me outside the Wells Fargo Building.

We stayed and took more pictures of the old antique's to the building. The place is peaceful. But at one time, it was like any other mining town, that grew to fast. It grabbed the attention of robbers.

And while it would definitely got robbed. Maybe in a shoot out, our little girl was shot. We left the building and started to walk around the side of it, where two holes penetrated the sand stone wall.

And as I was looking at the holes, I heard a voice: " tie the horses here!" " Tie the horsed up here." Then it was gone. We walked over to our car and got it. And we left the miner and the little girl, behind.

HARMONY

Eleven miles north from St. George, Utah on Interstate 15 is two shells of once was a home. The homes were built in the 1800's. When the Mormon pioneers moved into a small valley.

Unknown to them, they had settled where once laid the bodies of a great gang. The time period is long before America was discovered. During this time period, only Indians roamed the Americans. The name of the band of robbers is found in the Book of Mormon. The Gadiaton robbers were a secretive society.

Their evil remained behind. The pioneers love this small valley. Half way up the one side of the hill, leading to St. George. You can feel the heat of the southern, Utah sun. The other side of the valley is cooler. It was a perfect place to settle.

The Mormons used the sand stone to build their homes. The town was complete. They lived there quiet content. Their crops in the field grew in abundant. It seemed almost to good to be true. Little by little bickering started to grow in the small valley. Neighbor turned against neighbor, families turned on families. Fights broke out every day. No one really knew why? Word was sent to their leader. He came down to visit this small group of people.

Before he left, he told them to gather their belongings and move far away from this place. And told them, The Gadiation robbers of long ago, roamed this area and are more then likely buried here in this valley.

The pioneers did as he said. They packed their belongings and left the area. Over one hundred years has gone by, since they picked up their belongings and left. Up until about 20 years ago, the valley laid dormant.

The man who told us the story, had long since died. The young people at the church meeting has grown up, and forgotten the story once told us. The new town is now called Harrisburg. I've walked up to the houses, and have even taken pictures of them.

But what we captured on a DVD recorder was unbelievable. It sounds like two people fighting. Wind blowing on a calm day.

But can only be heard by the two homes. The area is not kept up, as it was when the town was built. It has a eerie feeling about it. It makes you wonder, if the evil that was there so long ago, had just stayed waiting for more people to come. So they may feed on their anger. I've only seen but a few people out of their homes, who to know what goes on.

Virgin River Hotel and Casino

I work at the Virgin River. I was hired to work in the slot department. I work in one of the two booths, giving change, buying buckets of nickels and quarters.

It was during one of these nights, that I was working in the north booth. That my new boss of only a month walked up to my booth, and asked me, " why?" Before I could ask why, what? He turned and left. My thoughts was that I had a idiot of a boss.

I didn't watch him leave the area, due to the fact I was getting customers at my front window. I went and didn't think any more about it. I came to work the next day, when we were all drawn into the slot office. And was told of Steve's death.

Steve, my boss lived in Las Vegas. Which is 90 miles southwest of Mesquite, Neveda. His house was broken into and he was killed. The Steve that I saw, while I was at the booth working, was already dead. Steve loved working at the Virgin River. His wife sold his house, and they moved away. No one knows for sure who killed him, only he did.

Employee Dinning Room at the Virgin River

The employee's room at the Virgin River are given meals at the edr. And its where everyone eats.

One night my co-worker Cathy and myself, was eating in the edr. We were sitting alone at one of the tables. When the condiments at the table started to move.

It was as if they had been alive on the table. It only went on for a few seconds, and then it all stopped as fast as it had started.

Both me and Cathy shook the table, trying to get the condiments to once again start to jump. But the harder we tried the worse we failed. When we stopped trying, Cathy finally said:" will you leave your ghost's at home!!" We both laughed, and returned to work. We haven't ate lunch together since it happened, almost two years ago.

Marty and Elizabeth

Marty and Elizabeth were in thei late 60's. They both worked for the casino for years. With their failing health, they were forced to quit. About a year after Marty quit, he came down with cancer. It was to far advanced for any cure to help Marty.

One day Marty came to me and asked, is there an after life? I told him, yes. That we do go on. After that I was transferred to the cage. It was the same work. Marty died.

About a week later, Rick the graveyard bar tender, went to the liqueur cabinet to get some liqueur. And there in the area stood Marty, smiling as always and then vanished. Rick told a few other people, that he had seen Marty. They told him to stop drinking on the job.

It was about a month after that, that I noticed Marty walking in our dead room. Its an area between two doors. The door to the casino, and the door to the soft count room. Where the money from the slot machines, are counted. Every once in a while my shirt is pulled at along with Cathy's shirt. I've often wondered who pulls on our shirts?

RAY

It had only been three months after Ray had died. That Liz had been in the Virgin River Restaurant waiting for me, to get off work and come in and join her for our lunch.

When she looked up, and there across the room was her dad. Walking towards her, until he saw her looking at him. He just disappeared into thin air.

It was a couple of weeks later, I was in the cage along with my supervisor. We were looking out at the front door, discussing something. I don't remember exactly. But there in a glare of the light, was Ray walking towards me. Smiling his funny little grin.

It was as if he wanted to say something, but my supervisor shook my arm. I didn't know I was even crying. I turned back, to where Ray was coming to me, and he was gone.

DICK

Its been two years since Liz worked in p.b.x. Where she would answer the incoming calls, to make reservations for the hotel room.

One morning when Liz arrived for work, she found only Eva working. Liz asked, " where's Karen?"" She had to leave to go take care of some business." As Liz was getting ready to go to work at her station.

Chris walked into the room. There standing behind Chris was Dick. Dick used to be a supervisor. But yet there he was, right behind Chris. Everyone knew that Dick was hopelessly in love with Chris.

Even though she was now married to her husband, Doug. Dick would follow Chris to hell and back. But would Chris? That was Dick following Chris.

Then as if someone had come up and threw gun oil down Liz's throat, she tasted gun oil.

Then gun smoke inflamed her nose, and she knew what had happened. Dick was dead, and he had killed himself.

A moment later Karen, walks back into the room. And told everyone that Dick had died. And that he had killed himself. She had told us, she had to identify his body.

Some construction worker had found Dick, on the side of a small hill that he could see his condo. He ahd laid out a blanket, so he wouldn't get his clothes dirty. He was always spotless dresser. Never a kinder man, you could of found. He left everything to Chris.

3210 East Cimarron Drive

The house at 3210 East Cimarron Drive is only four years old. We bought the home as it was still being built. We used to drive out to it after midnight, to see how it was coming.

Even in the early stages of construction, we could feel the unrest of the house being built.

Over on the road that runs through the town of Beaverdam, is the old road from Utah. It is also the old Spanish Trail. We live in the middle of the earth's lay lines. So it is why, this place deserves a chapter in this book? You decide.

The first few months that we lived in our brand new home. I woke in bed and raised up on my elbows to turn over, when a tall young boy passed my bed.

He was aboutsix feet tall, work coveralls, and a yellow and blue plaid cotton shirt. His hands were together in front of him, with his head slightly bowed. And had light brown to blonde hair. He slowly walked by the bed, and threw the wall.

That day I rearranged the bedroom. The bed is now in front of the windows, and I have not seen the young man since. Just shortly after the young man appearance, we started to get noises in the garage. We would go out there, but never found anything moved or out of place.

We would get the smell of coffee, and the occasional dog barking at the ceiling. But it wasn't until we came back from Texas, Connie's little trip to Jefferson. That we started to get the smell of cigar smoke.

We named him the cigar man. We smelled him in Jefferson, and he just followed us home. And so every so often we will get the brief smell of someone smoking a cigar.

Then came Christmas, and it was time to decorate the house. And we took pictures as Liz often does. And there I was putting up the decorations, and there they were, orbs of all sizes surrounding me.

The more pictures we took, the more orbs we caught. Then one night Krissy, came over to see us. And we were standing outside, saying good-bye. When something or someone walked by the bedroom curtain.

She verbally counted the heads, then stuttered so badly that we could harldy understand her. " There is somebody in your bedroom!!" We all looked at the bedroom window, and saw nothing there. " Krissy there is nothing there, except maybe a ghost. You know we have ghosts. Ther is nothing to be scared of." She left that night, and hasn't been back since.

Ray died on July 20, 2008. My bedroom is icy cold at all times. We could almost use it for a fridge, to keep the milk cold. It doesn't matter if I leave the doors open, it is still cold. Ray has been spotted at the Virgin River Restaurant, and in front of the cage.

He sits in his old chair in the bedroom at times. The kitchen cupboards open and close on their own.

We know he doesn't come to scare us. But he is here to check up on us.

Karen my sister, who died five years ago. Has also been seen peaking around the corner of the wall, watching us as we watch television.

It wouldn't matter where we live, the ghosts would follow us. Its apart of who we are. For we are, Darlene and Elizabeth (D.E.) Gould, will be FOREVER HAUNTED!!